HEALING FROM DIVORCE ~ 35 PRAYERS ROOTED IN GOD'S WORD FOR DIVORCED CHRISTIANS

Dana L Williams
www.redeemed-identity.com

Copyright 2025 Dana L Williams
Healing After Divorce:
35 Prayers Rooted In
God's Word For
Divorced Christians
Redeemed-Identity Publishing
©2025
Printed in the USA

ISBN Print: 979-8-9989508-0-3
ISBN Ebook: 979-8-9989508-1-0
Library of Congress Control Number: 2025910180
All rights reserved.

This book is protected under the copyright laws of the United States of America. Any reproduction or unauthorized use of the material or artwork contained herein is prohibited without the express written permission of Dana L Williams.

No part of this publication may be reproduced or transmitted in any form or by any means, electronic or mechanical, without permission in writing from the author.

Request for permission to make copies of any part of this work should be directed to the website: www.redeemed-identity.com.

Editor: Claudia Scott
Cover Art by: Maryna Zakharchuk
Formatting by: Desiree Young

Scripture quotations taken from the New King James Version unless specified differently. Scripture taken from the New King James Version®. Copyright © 1982 by Thomas Nelson. Used by permission. All rights reserved.

Scripture quotations marked (ESV) are from the ESV® Bible (The Holy Bible, English Standard Version®), copyright © 2001 by Crossway, a publishing ministry of Good News Publishers. Used by permission. All rights reserved.

Contents

Endorsements

Acknowledgements

Why Prayers for Divorced Christians? 9

<u>Part I. Prayers for Emotional Healing 12</u>

Prayers for When You Are Angry 13

Prayers for When You Don't Feel Worthy 16

Prayers for When You Don't Feel You Can Trust the Lord 19

Prayers for When You're Fearful About Provision 23

Prayers for When You Feel Abandoned 26

Prayers for When You Feel Bitter 29

Prayers for When You Feel Fearful 32

Prayers for When You Feel Like a Failure 35

Prayers for When You Feel Sad, Pressed, And Empty 38

Prayers for When You Feel Weak 42

Prayers for When You Are Filled with Anxiety 45

Prayers for When Hope Seems Far Away 47

Prayers for When Need God to Redeem Your Pain 51

Prayers for When You Need Healing 54

Prayers for When Pain Feels Too Deep 57

Prayers for When You Struggle With Rejection 60

Prayers for When You Struggle With Shame 63

Prayers for When You're Weary of Crying 66

Part II. Prayers for Family 69

Prayers for When Your Children Need Healing 70

Prayers for When You Pray For Healing Over Your Former Spouse 73

Prayers for When You Worried About Your Children 76

Part III. Prayers for Forgiveness 79

Prayers for When Forgiveness Feels Impossible 80

Prayers for When You're Offended With God 83

Prayers for When Unforgiveness Feels Good 86

Prayers for When Want to Take Justice Into Your Own Hands 89

Part IV. Prayers for Identity 92

Prayers for When You Don't Remember Who You Are 93

Prayers for When You Feel Disqualified 96

Prayers for When You Struggle to Accept God's Love 99

Prayers for When You Struggle With Your Identity in Christ 103

Part V. Prayers for Spiritual Warfare 106

Prayers for Recovery After Abuse 107

Prayers for When You Need To War For Your Children 110

Prayers for When You Need to War Over Your Heart 113

Prayers for When You Need To War For Your Future 117

Prayers for When You Need to Build Boundaries Around Your Heart 121

Prayers for When You Need To Engage in Spiritual Warfare 124

A Free Resource for You 127

About the Author 128

Where to find Dana L. Wiliams and Redeemed-Identity 130

ENDORSEMENTS

Dana Williams has utilized Scripture to create a guide for those going through or recovering from divorce. Her keen insight has brought helpful meditations for many of the struggles faced by those in recovery. from this devastating circumstance. There are questions to ponder and decrees for going forward. You will find help and healing in the pages of Dana's book. I have been divorced for many years and yet I found new insights as I edited the book. I know you will be blessed by this book.

C.J. Scott
Award winning author, Editor

This devotional is a sacred companion for anyone wrestling with difficult emotions or life transitions. The prayers, reflections, and declarations will guide your heart gently back to God's love, truth, and healing presence.

Loren Cribbs
Author of *Wings to Rise Above Divorce*, #1 Best Seller on Amazon
https://www.lorencribbs.com/divorcedevo

Dana Williams has created a gentle yet truth-telling companion for every woman piecing her life together after divorce. I was especially moved by the section that dares to name what few of us admit aloud—those moments when we feel angry or even offended by God. Dana meets us there without judgment, showing that honesty is the first step toward healing.

Each devotion is beautifully bite-sized, but none of them skim the surface. The prayers breathe hope, the reflection questions dig deep enough to unearth buried pain, and the bold faith declarations lift our eyes to what's still possible with God. I closed the final page feeling seen, strengthened, and ready to keep walking in joy.

If your heart is tender and your faith feels fragile, this book will steady your steps.

Yvette Walker,
Host of the Positively Joy podcast
Founder of Positively Joy Ministries,
www.positivelyjoy.com

ACKNOWLEDGEMENTS

First and foremost, I want to give praise to my Savior for bringing me out of darkness and into His marvelous light. Without Him, I am nothing. Your unending grace, guidance, and love have made this book possible. You have been my refuge and my strength, my source of healing and restoration, and I give You all the glory.

To my children, Kyle and Hannah, thank you for being a source of immense encouragement and unconditional love throughout my years of healing and stepping into my calling. Your presence in my life is a constant reminder of God's blessings, and I am so grateful for you.

To my GNO (Girls Night Out) friends and my covenant "California" friends, I could not have done any of this without your love, laughter, drying my tears, and praying me whole. I love you all deeply, and your friendship has been a lifeline.

To my friends and mentors, therapist, Peggy Hurd, thank you for walking alongside me, listening without judgment, and offering words of wisdom and hope. Your presence in my life has been a gift, and your faith in me has kept me going.

To the incredible community of believers who have inspired and uplifted me, thank you for your faith-filled stories, testimonies, and prayers. You have reminded me of the power of God's promises and the beauty of His faithfulness.

To the readers of this book, I want to express my deepest gratitude. Thank you for allowing me to share this part of my journey with you. My hope and prayer is that these prayers will bring you closer to God and guide you toward healing and renewal.

Finally, to every person who encouraged me to write this book, thank you for believing in the calling God has placed on my life. Your words of affirmation have been a light in the moments of doubt, and your support has been invaluable.

May this book be a testament to God's amazing grace, and may it bless and strengthen each person who reads it.

Why Prayers for Divorced Christians?

Divorce is a sandstorm, relentless and disorienting, stirring up fear, shame, and countless questions. It tears through your life like a torrential cyclone, leaving you searching for clarity and strength. In those moments, even prayer can feel impossible. I know this because I've been there. There were countless days when I simply sat in silence, unable to find the words to pray. That is why I wrote this book.

The Word of God has an answer for every heartache, pain, and fear. It is our lighthouse in the divorce darkness. Within these pages, you will find 35 prayers rooted directly in Scripture, designed to address some of the most common struggles during and after divorce. This book is not an exhaustive resource but serves as a launching pad into your new life, helping you reconnect with God's promises and rebuild your faith.

Praying the Word of God is powerful. As I shared in my free eBook, "Who Am I After Divorce?" When I started praying specific Scriptures about my identity in Christ OVER myself, out loud, it took on abundant life. I, spiritually and emotionally, took ownership of God's love letters to me. It was as if He was speaking these Scriptures directly over me. They became a personal love letter from God to me as I declared them aloud over myself.

When we pray the Word, we are wielding a powerful weapon against the darkness. The Bible is filled with promises and truths about our identity and destiny as children of God. By praying these truths aloud, we replace the lies we believe about ourselves—or the hurtful words of others—with God-breathed declarations. This transforms us from the inside out, renewing our minds and igniting our spirits with His truth and love.

This book is designed to help you experience this transformation. Each prayer is accompanied by three *Reflection Questions* and three *Declarations* to help you dive deeper into your journey with God. These tools will guide you to uncover hidden areas where He desires to bring healing and renewal. The Declarations are crafted to replace the destructive narratives that may echo in your heart and mind, empowering you to embrace God's truth. Additionally, blank, lined pages are included for your personal prayers, favorite scripture from this prayer and notes as the Lord meets you in these moments.

As you work through these prayers and reflections, I encourage you to speak them aloud. It might feel unfamiliar at first, but your soul is thirsty to hear the Word of God. Speaking His truth aloud allows it to resonate deeply within you, bringing clarity, hope, and strength.

Through these prayers, you'll discover how God's promises can replace pain with peace, fear with faith, and despair with hope. He is ready to meet you where you are, to heal your heart, and to lead you into the abundant life He has planned for you.

Like a lighthouse guiding you through the storm, God's Word will lead you to hope, peace, and joy. May this book be a beacon for you as you step into healing and renewal.

*Now may the God of hope fill you with all joy and peace in believing,
that you may abound in hope by the power of the Holy Spirit.*
Romans 15:13 (NKJV)

PRAYERS FOR EMOTIONAL HEALING

Prayers for When You Are Angry

Jesus, I am so grateful for your mercy and grace. I am so thankful that you are slow to anger, and you abound in steadfast and unending love. I come to you with this anger. It weighs me down like an anchor around my neck. I do not want to be rash with my mouth, and I do not want my heart to utter anything unpleasing to you. But my humanity gets in the way and trips me up.

Forgive me for harboring anger and rage. Forgive me for my words of anger. I long to be quick to hear and slow to speak. I do not want to express words of anger toward anyone because it does not produce your righteousness. Help me to set boundaries and share pain righteously and not out of rage. Help my words to be few.

Holy Spirit, help me to bring any anger to your footstool as I feel it rising. Keep me from being provoked in my spirit, for it is written in your Word that anger resides in the hearts of fools. Teach me not to take to heart hurtful words of others, knowing that I am responsible for my own reply to them. Help me to overlook offense and not let harsh words take root in my soul.

It is written in Ephesians; be angry but not sin. Let me not hold onto anger, but release it before the sun sets, so that I give no foothold to the enemy.

In Jesus' name,

Amen

REFLECTION QUESTIONS

1. How do you usually respond when you feel anger rising, and in what ways can you invite the Holy Spirit to help handle those emotions before they lead to sin?
2. In what areas of your life have you been holding onto anger, and how can you take steps to release it to God rather than allowing it to weigh you down?
3. Are you allowing the hurtful words or actions of others to take root in your heart? How can you respond in a way that reflects Christ's love and grace instead of reacting in anger?

_____

_____

_____

_____

_____

_____

_____

DECLARATIONS

1. I declare that I will bring all my anger to God's footstool, allowing the Holy Spirit to guide my responses, and I will not let anger lead me into sin.
2. I declare that I will release any anger or offense weighing on my heart, trusting in God's grace to

free me and choosing to walk in peace and forgiveness.
3. I declare that I will not let the hurtful words or actions of others take root in my soul, but instead, I will respond with the love and patience of Christ, allowing His righteousness to shine through me.

SCRIPTURE REFERENCES

James 1:19-20
Ecclesiastes 5:2
Ecclesiastes 7:9
Ecclesiastes 7:21
Ephesians 4:26-27
Psalm 103:8-12
Proverbs 15:1

Journal/Notes: Pick one of the above scriptures, write it out and reflect on how you can put it into operation in your life today.

_____
_____
_____
_____
_____
_____
_____

Prayers for When You Don't Feel Worthy

I remind my body, soul and spirit that I am His workmanship. I am created in Christ Jesus for good works, which my God prepared beforehand so that I would walk in them victoriously. It is written that I am the adopted child of the highest God and I will not fear because Christ has redeemed me and He calls me by name!

I remind the enemy that I belong to God. _He_ calls me worthy. _He_ calls me beloved child. _He_ died for me so that I might spend eternity with Him. _He_ calls me His own. So, spirit of low self-worth, insecurity, shame, be gone in Jesus' Name! I was bought with a sacred and holy price – the blood of Christ because HE calls me worthy!

Thank you, Jesus, that I am a part of Your chosen generation, a royal priest in Your Kingdom. I am Your special child. I praise you, Lord, because you called me out of darkness and brought me into Your marvelous light. Thank you for calling me worthy. Thank you for declaring your love over me. Thank you for marking me and sealing me for redemption.

In Christ's precious name...the name above all names, Jesus...amen

REFLECTION QUESTIONS

1. In what ways can you embrace your identity as God's beloved child, created for a purpose, especially in moments of self-doubt or fear?
2. What are the specific areas in your life where you struggle with these feelings? How can you actively reject these negative perceptions and

replace them with the truth that you are worthy and beloved by God?
3. How does the knowledge that you are a member of His chosen generation and royal priesthood impact the way you live your daily life? In what ways can you reflect this royal and chosen identity in your actions, decisions, and relationships with others?

_____

_____

_____

_____

_____

_____

_____

DECLARATIONS

1. I was purchased with a great price. This proves to me and to the enemy my worth.
2. I am worthy because HE says I am worthy. I will not listen to others that say otherwise.
3. I am a child of the King of Kings! He called me out of darkness and into HIS light!

SCRIPTURE REFERENCES
1 Peter 2:9
Ephesians 2:10

Ephesians 1:5
Isaiah 43:1
1 Peter 2:9
Luke 12:7

Journal/Notes: Pick one of the above scriptures, write it out and reflect on how you can put it into operation in your life today.

_____

_____

_____

_____

_____

_____

_____

Prayers for When You Don't Feel You Can Trust the Lord

Lord, my heart is heavy, and I feel crushed by the rejection I've faced from those who call themselves your people. The pain of being judged and misunderstood by others has shaken my trust, and I wrestle with placing my confidence in You. Yet, Your Word calls me to trust in You with all my heart and to lean not on my own understanding. Help me surrender my pain, my questions, and my doubts to You. Show me how to acknowledge You in all my ways, trusting that You will make my path straight, even when others push me aside.

When fear tries to overwhelm me, I will choose to remember Your promises. When I am afraid, I will trust in You. In You, whose Word I praise, I place my trust. What can mere mortals do to me when You, the eternal God, are my protector and refuge?

You have said, "Do not fear, for I am with You; do not be dismayed, for I am Your God." Lord, I hold onto this truth. You strengthen me, help me, and uphold me with Your righteous right hand. Even when the rejection stings and the loneliness feels unbearable, I will cling to the knowledge that You are with me, sustaining me in my weakness.

I know Your plans for me are good, Lord. Even though this season feels so hard, I trust that You have plans to prosper me, not to harm me, and to give me hope and a future. You are not the author of rejection or shame, but the author of love, restoration, and redemption.

Lord, You are my strength and my shield; my heart trusts in You, and You help me. Though others may fail me, You never will. My heart leaps for joy, and with my song, I will praise You because You are faithful, even when others are not. Thank You for loving me unconditionally, for being my refuge in the storm, and for walking with me every step of this journey.

In Jesus' name,

Amen.

REFLECTION QUESTIONS

1. How can you let go of the pain of rejection from others and focus on trusting God's plan for your life, even when it feels uncertain?
2. In what ways can you remind yourself of God's constant presence and promises when fear or doubt begins to overwhelm you?
3. How can you shift your perspective from relying on the opinions of others to leaning fully on God's truth and love for you?

_____

_____

_____

_____

_____

DECLARATIONS

1. I declare that I will trust in the Lord with all my heart and lean not on my own understanding, for He is directing my path.
2. I declare that I will not fear or be dismayed, for God is my strength, my helper, and my refuge, and He upholds me with His righteous hand.
3. I declare that God's plans for my life are good, filled with hope and a future, and no rejection or judgment from others can take that away.

SCRIPTURE REFERENCES

Proverbs 3:5-7
Psalm 56:3-4
Isaiah 41:10
Jeremiah 29:11
Psalm 28:7

Journal/Notes: Pick one of the above scriptures, write it out and reflect on how you can put it into operation in your life today.

Prayers for When You're Fearful About Provision

Jesus, You are my sun and shield! You provide grace and glory from your heavens. It is written in your word that you will not withhold any good thing from those who walk uprightly. I will seek first your kingdom and Your righteousness and all the things I need will be added to me. I am your child, and you will not allow me to go hungry and you will come against the wickedness that is against me.

You, alone, are my rock, my fortress and my deliverer. You are my strength when I have none and I trust in you alone. Not my bank account, my job, my former spouse...only you. For you are my provider and my stronghold. Hallelujah!

I will not fear bad news because my heart is fastened securely on you and your throne room. Your thoughts toward me are good and not evil to give me a future and a hope, and this includes provision. Jesus, you are more than enough. You give immeasurably more than I ask or imagine, according to Your power that is at work within me, to Him be the glory!

In Jesus' name...amen.

REFLECTION QUESTIONS

1. In what areas of your life do you struggle to trust God's provision? How can you shift your focus from relying on worldly sources of security (like

money, job, or relationships) to trusting fully in God as your provider?
2. What steps can you take to keep your heart and mind focused on God's promises of protection and provision, especially during difficult times?
3. What changes might you need to make in your routine, decisions, or mindset to align more closely with this principle?

_____

_____

_____

_____

_____

_____

_____

DECLARATIONS

1. I release my dependence on worldly security and choose to trust fully in God's abundant provision for every area of my life.
2. I choose to stand on God's promises of protection and provision, knowing He is faithful through every trial.
3. I seek first the kingdom of God in all that I do. I will align my choices, actions, and thoughts with His will and purpose for my life.

SCRIPTURES REFERENCES

Psalm 84:11
Matthew 6:33
Proverbs 10:3
Psalm 18:2
Psalm 112:7 (NIV)
Jeremiah 29:11
Ephesians 3:20 (NIV)

Journal/Notes: Pick one of the above scriptures, write it out and reflect on how you can put it into operation in your life today.

_____

_____

_____

_____

_____

_____

_____

Prayers for When You Feel Abandoned

Lord, your Word tells me to be strong and of good courage and not feel afraid. But some days, especially when I feel forsaken by the people I love, I just hurt too much to feel anything but lost and alone. It is times like this that I choose to remind my heart that God goes with me everywhere and He will not leave me or abandon me.

Jesus, I put my trust in you because you have not nor will not ever forsake me, leave me, or ignore me. You promise to be with me to the end of the age. Even when it feels like I have lost so much during this season, it is written that you will not forsake me or my inheritance because my inheritance is in You.

I turn my heart and hurt toward You and ask you to help me feel your presence. Wrap your arms around my broken heart and bind my wounds, for you, alone, heal my pain and comfort me as I grieve.

I thank you in advance for the healing work You have begun in me. Thank you for being with me always and never leaving or forsaking me.

In Jesus' precious name...amen.

REFLECTION QUESTIONS

1. When you feel abandoned or hurt, how can you remind myself of God's constant presence?
2. How does trusting in God as your inheritance bring comfort during seasons of loss and grief?

3. What steps can you take to open your heart to God's healing and allow His love to mend your wounds?

_____
_____
_____
_____
_____
_____
_____

DECLARATIONS

1. I trust that God is always with me—He will never leave me nor forsake me, no matter how I feel.
2. My inheritance is secure in Christ, and even in loss, I find hope and comfort in Him.
3. God's healing power is at work within me, and His love surrounds and strengthens my heart each day.

SCRIPTURE REFERENCES

Deuteronomy 31:6
Psalm 9:10
Matthew 28:20
Psalm 94:14
Matthew 28:20
Deuteronomy 4:30-31

Psalm 147:3

Journal/Notes: Pick one of the above scriptures, write it out and reflect on how you can put it into operation in your life today.

_____

_____

_____

_____

_____

_____

_____

Prayers for When You Feel Bitter

Lord, I am struggling! I am hurt, angry, and bitter. I try not to be but I need your help. Your word says that we are to bear with one another and not have a complaint against another and that we are supposed to forgive as you forgive. But I feel like all I do is complain about (their name here)_____. I am so sorry. I need to be quick to listen and slow to speak. Even more so, I need to be slow to anger because it does not produce your righteousness. Forgive me Lord.

In Jesus' name, I choose to put away all bitterness and wrath. I want to be tender hearted, and I want to forgive as Christ forgave me. I command a spirit of bitterness to leave, in Jesus' mighty name. Lord, I do not want to be defiled by the bitterness I feel that I carry in my heart. I need to ask for Your grace toward _____. As hard as it is, Lord, I choose not to react, respond, and do any acts of vengeance or even speak vengeance toward them. I want to be an example of your grace to all those around me.

Jesus, I can only do this under the power of Your Holy Spirit. I choose to drink from your well of grace, and not a well of bitterness. Holy Spirit, remind me when I dip my cup in that bitter well, and remind me to dip my cup from the well of your grace.

In Jesus' name,

Amen

REFLECTION QUESTIONS

1. What kind of situations stir up bitterness in you?
2. Is there a way that you can avoid these situations, i.e. only communicate in email so you can reflect on your words?
3. When do you find it hardest to extend grace, and how can you rely on the Holy Spirit to guide your reactions in those moments?

_____

_____

_____

_____

_____

_____

_____

DECLARATIONS

1. I declare that I will walk in forgiveness and release bitterness, choosing grace over anger.
2. I command every spirit of wrath, bitterness, and resentment to leave my heart in Jesus' name.
3. With the help of the Holy Spirit, I will respond with tenderness and love, because I want to be an example of God's grace to those around me.

SCRIPTURE REFERENCES

Colossians 3:13
James 1:19-20
Ephesians 4:31–32
1 John 2:9
Psalm 37:8
Romans 12:19

Journal/Notes: Pick one of the above scriptures, write it out and reflect on how you can put it into operation in your life today.

_____

_____

_____

_____

_____

_____

_____

Prayers for When You Feel Fearful

Lord, sometimes it feels like fear is overtaking me at every turn. I know your Word says I shouldn't feel afraid, but some days it just too big. So, I will remind my heart and soul that Your Word tells me in Isaiah 41 that you are with me and that I am not to feel dismayed or afraid. You promised that You will strengthen me, help me and hold me up with Your righteous right hand. Even though I walk through the darkest of valleys, I will choose to fear no evil because you are with me, and your rod and staff will comfort and protect me.

Jesus, you are my refuge and my strength during this time. Therefore, by faith, I declare over my heart and soul that I will not fear even though things around me give away and fall apart, I will not fear because You are with me.

In Psalms, it says that you are with me and to not be afraid for what can mere humans do to me! Sometimes it feels like humans can do the most damage. But I know that you are with me during these times. Lord, I reach for your peace. I literally and figuratively lift my hand to you and reach for that peace that you promise me.

In Jesus' name, I come against fear and all its chaos. I command fear to bow to the Lordship of Jesus Christ and the Word of God. You have no permanent dwelling place in my soul. I am a child of the most-high God, and I was bought with His blood that protects me.

In Jesus powerful name, amen.

REFLECTION QUESTIONS

1. What specific fears are you currently facing, and how do they impact your daily life?
2. When life feels chaotic and uncertain, where do you typically seek refuge? How can you more intentionally turn to God as your primary source of strength and peace during challenging times?
3. What steps can you take to resist the chaos of fear and embrace the security that comes from being a child of the living God?

_____

_____

_____

_____

_____

_____

_____

DECLARATIONS

1. I will not be overtaken by fear, for God strengthens me, helps me, and upholds me with His righteous right hand.
2. Even when life falls apart, I will not fear, for God is my refuge, my strength, and my ever-present help.

3. Fear has no place in my soul—I stand in the peace of Christ, knowing I am protected and covered by His blood.

SCRIPTURE REFERENCES

Isaiah 41:10
Psalm 23:4
Psalm 27:1
Psalm 46:1-3
Psalm 118:6
John 14:27

Journal/Notes: Pick one of the above scriptures, write it out and reflect on how you can put it into operation in your life today.

_____

_____

_____

_____

_____

_____

_____

Prayers for When You Feel Like a Failure

Father, I come to You feeling weighed down by my mistakes and feeling like I've failed you and my family. I am discouraged and ashamed, struggling to see past my failures. Yet, I know that You are a God of mercy and compassion, who understands my struggles and loves me as I am.

Lord, remind me that my worth is not defined by my failures but by Your love and purpose for my life. Help me to see this season as part of my growth, a step toward the future You have prepared for me. Strengthen me to rise each time I fall and to press forward, knowing that You are working in me and will complete the good work You started.

Thank You for holding me up when I stumble and for guiding me through this with your patience. Help me to forgive myself, to learn from my mistakes, and to trust in Your grace and direction. Change me, Lord, so I reflect your Truth and Grace in my life. I surrender my doubts and insecurities to You, and I choose to believe that I am not a failure in this divorce season—I am a child of God, walking toward Your promises.

In Jesus' name, Amen.

REFLECTION QUESTIONS

1. How can seeing failure as part of God's growth process help bring encouragement and hope?
2. In what ways might trusting in God's plan provide reassurance and strength after a divorce?

3. How does knowing that God is patient and compassionate help you to forgive yourself and keep moving forward?

_____

_____

_____

_____

_____

_____

_____

DECLARATIONS

1. I am not defined by my failures or divorce; I am a child of God, and He is working in me.
2. When I fall, I will rise again, for the Lord upholds me with His hand.
3. I am confident that God will complete the good work He has started in me.

SCRIPTURE REFERENCES

Proverbs 24:16
Philippians 3:12
Psalm 37:23-24
Philippians 1:6
Psalm 103:13

Journal/Notes: Pick one of the above scriptures, write it out and reflect on how you can put it into operation in your life today.

_____
_____
_____
_____
_____
_____
_____

Prayers for When You Sad, Pressed, and Empty

Heavenly Father, I come before You, grateful for Your presence in my life. Your Word reminds me in that You are my salvation, my strength, and my song. In times of sorrow and emptiness, I declare my trust in You, knowing that You will fill me with joy as I draw from the wells of Your salvation.

Lord, I thank You for hearing the cries of the broken-hearted. It is written, that when I struggle with sadness and depression, I can rest in the knowledge that You are near. You will deliver me from my troubles. You lift me up when I cannot lift myself. You are my shield and my glory, the One who lifts my head high when I feel low.

I take comfort in Your plans for my future. You have thoughts of peace toward me, to give me hope and a future, even when I can't yet see it. Lord, I believe that You will turn my mourning into joy and bring comfort to my soul. I rejoice in the knowledge that You are at work, transforming my sorrow into songs of praise.

Jesus, help me delight in Your Word. I want to be like a tree planted by rivers of water, nourished by Your truth, bearing fruit in due season, and flourishing even during hardship. Let everything I do prosper, as I root myself in Your promises.

Finally, Lord, I ask You to help me fix my mind on what is true, noble, pure, and lovely. In moments of doubt, fill my thoughts with Your goodness, and let me meditate on all that is praiseworthy. Thank You for being the lifter of my head, the healer of my heart, and the source of my strength.

I praise You for all the excellent things You have done and are going to do that I can't see yet. I give You all the glory.

In Jesus' mighty name, Amen.

REFLECTIVE QUESTIONS

1. In what areas of your life are you struggling to trust in God's strength and salvation, and how can you invite Him to be your shield and lifter of your head during this season?
2. How are you currently handling moments of brokenness or sadness? Are you turning to God and His promises for comfort and healing?
3. What can you meditate on today that is true, noble, pure, and lovely to help shift your focus from your struggles to God's goodness and peace?

_____

_____

_____

_____

_____

_____

_____

DECLARATIONS

1. I declare that God is my strength, my salvation, and my shield. I will not be afraid, for He is the One who lifts my head and fills my soul with joy.
2. I declare that God has good plans for me—plans of peace, hope, and a future. He is turning my mourning into joy and bringing comfort to my heart.
3. I declare that my mind will focus on what is true, noble, pure, and praiseworthy. I will meditate on God's goodness and trust in His faithful promises for my life.

SCRIPTURE REFERENCES

Isaiah 12:2-6
Psalm 1: 2-3
Psalm 34:17-18
Jeremiah 29:11
Jeremiah 31:13
Psalm 3:3
Philippians 4:8

Journal/Notes: Pick one of the above scriptures, write it out and reflect on how you can put it into operation in your life today.

_____

_____

_____

_____

_____
_____
_____

Prayers for When You Feel Weak

Lord, I feel weak today. Weak and tired. I seek you and your strength. I seek your face beg for transformation as I renew my mind with your Word. I remember your miracles and blessings you've granted me in the past. I choose to remind my soul of your wonders and your strength. I remind my soul and spirit that your mercies are new every day and Your compassion will never fail me. Your faithfulness has seen me through many trials, and I need to cling to you because you are my portion, and my hope is in You alone.

I choose to not remember the former old things. I know you are doing a new thing in me. I don't want to miss the road in the wilderness and the river in the desert. Show me where the road is, Jesus. Bring me to the river in this painful desert so that I can be revived and refreshed. It is written that you have thoughts of peace toward me and that I have a future. Your Word says you store up hope for me in heaven. I need some of that now.

Lord, you promise to renew my strength as I wait on you. You promise that I shall mount up with wings like eagles, that I will run and not be weary, and walk and not faint. So, I wait on you in your presence. Strengthen me as I worship you.

In your strong name, Jesus...amen

REFLECTION QUESTIONS

1. When you feel physically, emotionally, or spiritually drained, how can you intentionally seek God's strength and guidance? What practical steps can you take to renew your mind with His Word?
2. In what areas of your life do you need to let go of the past to fully embrace the new road God is laying before you?
3. What does it mean for you to "mount up with wings like eagles" in the context of your current circumstances?

_____

_____

_____

_____

_____

_____

_____

DECLARATIONS

1. When I feel drained, I will seek God's strength and renew my mind through His Word, trusting Him to guide me step by step.
2. I release the past and embrace this new path God is creating for me, staying open to His opportunities and direction.

3. As I wait in God's presence, I receive His renewal and rise above my circumstances, mounting up with wings like eagles.

SCRIPTURES

1 Chronicles 16:11-12
Lamentations 3:22-24
Isaiah 43:18-19
Jeremiah 29:11
Isaiah 40:31

Journal/Notes: Pick one of the above scriptures, write it out and reflect on how you can put it into operation in your life today.

_____

_____

_____

_____

_____

_____

_____

Prayers for When You Are Filled with Anxiety

Heavenly Father, I come to You right now, feeling so much anxiety in my heart. I am overwhelmed by worries and anxious thoughts, and I need Your strength and peace to fill me. I acknowledge that You are my refuge and my protector, and I choose to place my trust in You.

Lord, I ask You to drive out anxiety and fear and replace it with Your perfect love. Remind me that I am not alone, that You are with me, guiding and guarding me. Surround my dwelling with your angelic host to watch over me. It is written, You are my helper. I will not fear or allow anxiety to master me; for what can man do to me? Help me to see beyond my anxiety, to find courage in Your promises, and to hold onto the truth that You are my stronghold.

You have not given me a spirit of fear or anxiety, but of power, love, and a sound mind. I claim this truth over my life. I reject every anxious thought, and I embrace Your peace that surpasses all understanding. Thank You, Father, for being my light and my salvation, the One who lifts me up and keeps me safe.

In Jesus' Powerful Name, Amen.

REFLECTION QUESTIONS

1. Does your trust in God's presence and protection help calm anxious thoughts? If not, why?
2. What does it mean to embrace a spirit of "power, love, and a sound (calm) mind" instead of a anxiety?

3. How can remembering God as a stronghold provide strength and courage when feeling overwhelmed?

_____

_____

_____

_____

_____

_____

_____

DECLARATIONS

1. I am filled with God's power, love, and a sound mind; anxiety has no hold on me.
2. God is my refuge and my strength; I will not be afraid or anxious.
3. I trust in God's promises, and I am protected, safe, and choose to be at peace.

SCRIPTURE REFERENCES

Isaiah 41:10
Psalm 23:4
2 Timothy 1:7
Psalm 27:1
Hebrews 13:6
Psalm 34:4-5
Psalm 91:4-5

Journal/Notes: Pick one of the above scriptures, write it out and reflect on how you can put it into operation in your life today.

_____

_____

_____

_____

_____

_____

_____

Prayers for When Hope Seems Far Away

Heavenly Father, I come before You in need of Your hope. I ask, that You would give me the spirit of wisdom and revelation in the knowledge of You, that the eyes of my understanding may be enlightened, so that I may know the hope of Your calling. Lord, I need to be reminded of the riches of Your glory and the exceeding greatness of Your power toward me as a believer.

I hold onto Your promise, knowing that hope does not disappoint because Your love has been poured out in my heart by the Holy Spirit. Even when I feel uncertain or weighed down, I trust in Your plan for my life, and that You have thoughts of peace and not of evil, to give me a future and a hope.

My Jesus, I ask that You fill me with all joy and peace in believing, so that I may abound in hope by the power of the Holy Spirit. Renew my strength, Lord, for I will wait on You and trust that I will mount up with wings like eagles, I will run and not be weary, I will walk and not faint.

Jesus you are my HOPE. You are my anchor. You are firm and secure, even when my emotions are not.

In Jesus' Name...amen

REFLECTION QUESTIONS

1. How can you invite the spirit of wisdom and revelation into your life to deepen your understanding of God's calling for you?
2. In what ways can you anchor yourself in the hope and power of Christ, especially during times when your emotions feel unstable?
3. What can you do each day to remind yourself that your hope is in Christ?

_____

_____

_____

_____

_____

_____

_____

DECLARATIONS

1. I declare that I am filled with the spirit of wisdom and revelation, and my understanding is enlightened to fully know God's purpose and calling for my life.
2. I declare that Christ is my anchor and my hope, and I stand firm in Him, regardless of my emotions or circumstances.

3. I declare that I walk in the exceeding greatness of God's power, knowing that I am an heir to His promises and eternal inheritance.

SCRIPTURE REFERENCES

Ephesians 1:16-23
Romans 5:5
Jeremiah 29:11
Romans 15:13
Isaiah 40:31

Journal/Notes: Pick one of the above scriptures, write it out and reflect on how you can put it into operation in your life today.

_____
_____
_____
_____
_____
_____
_____

Prayers for When Need God to Redeem Your Pain

Heavenly Father, You know my tears and the burdens I carry. Your Word says, You have collected my tears in bottles and recorded them in Your book. I am weary from crying, but I hold onto the promise that You see my every tear, and none of them are wasted. I cling to the hope in that You promise to wipe away every tear from my eyes, and there will be no more death, sorrow, or pain, for You are making all things new.

In the midst of my weariness, I look to You, for as Psalm 46:1 says, you are my refuge and strength, a very present help in times of trouble. You are near to the broken-hearted, and You save those who are crushed in spirit. I feel crushed in my spirit, Lord. My soul feels faint and weary. Your Word promises you satisfy the longing soul and fill the hungry soul with goodness

I will not fear, for You have chosen me and called me by name. You are with me, You strengthen me, and You uphold me with Your righteous right hand. Lord, I trust You to renew my strength and lift the weight of my tears. Thank You for Your unending comfort and faithfulness.

In Jesus' mighty name...amen.

REFLECTION QUESTIONS

1. What does it mean to you to return to God's stronghold?

2. Make a list of your dreams that you felt died as a result of your divorce?
3. What areas are you struggling with fear?

_____

_____

_____

_____

_____

_____

_____

DECLARATIONS

1. I declare that God has collected my tears and will comfort me, wiping away all sorrow as He makes all things new.
2. I declare that God is my refuge and strength, and I trust Him to sustain me in my weariness and restore my soul.
3. I declare that I am upheld by God's righteous right hand, and I will not fear, for He strengthens me and is always with me.

SCRIPTURE REFERENCES

Psalm 71:20
Joel 2:25-26
Zechariah 9:12

1 Peter 5:10
Psalm 34:18
2 Cor 4:16-18

Journal/Notes: Pick one of the above scriptures, write it out and reflect on how you can put it into operation in your life today.

_____

_____

_____

_____

_____

_____

_____

Prayers for When You Need Healing

Lord, I come before You, feeling the weight of both physical and emotional wounds from this season of my life. My heart feels broken, and my body weary, as I process all the pain, loss, and change. Father, I ask You to be my Healer, to mend the places in me that are hurt and restore my strength.

Touch my heart, Lord, and bring peace to my mind. Let Your love spill into every empty space and bring comfort and peace where there is sorrow. Heal the pain that lingers and renew my hope for the future. Help me to release any bitterness or regret and to lean on You fully, trusting that You are restoring me emotionally and physically each day. Heal the physical effects these emotions have had on me.

Give me the strength to face each day with courage, and help me to see myself through Your eyes, whole and loved. I surrender my burdens and my healing process into Your hands, knowing that You are faithful. Thank You for being with me in this journey, for holding me up when I feel weak, and for the promise that You will renew and restore me.

In Jesus' Mighty name,

Amen.

REFLECTION QUESTIONS

1. How does trusting in God's power to heal bring comfort during times of physical and emotional pain?
2. How can you release bitterness or regret to embrace healing and restoration?
3. In what way can you focus on God's promises of hope for a renewed future after divorce?

_____

_____

_____

_____

_____

_____

_____

DECLARATIONS

1. I am healed and restored by God's love and grace.
2. I release my pain, bitterness, and regret, trusting God to fill me with peace.
3. I am renewed and strengthened each day by God's promises and faithfulness.

SCRIPTURE REFERENCES

Jeremiah 30:17
Isaiah 53:5

Exodus 15:26
Jeremiah 17:14
Psalm 103:2-3
Psalm 30:2

Journal/Notes: Pick one of the above scriptures, write it out and reflect on how you can put it into operation in your life today.

_____

_____

_____

_____

_____

_____

Prayers for When Pain Feels Too Deep

Jesus, I am so thankful that You hear each prayer and put my many tears in bottles, and You lovingly write my prayers and wanderings in Your books in heaven. It is written in your Word that You hear EVERY prayer of Your righteous children, and you deliver me from my troubles. Sometimes it doesn't feel like that Lord, but I know that your timing is different than mine. Thank you for being my refuge and strength. Thank you for being my help in these painful seasons.
You have chosen me as your child. You do not push me away. I choose to not allow fear to settle in my soul because You are with me. In Jesus name, I will not allow fear to speak into my life. I will not allow anxiety to capture me because YOU are my God and Your Word declares over me that You will strengthen me and will hold me up with Your righteous right hand. Jesus, I choose to not lose heart, even though my tears seem ever-present. It feels like I am wasting way on the inside; yet your Word promises me that You renew me day by day. For this momentary trouble and pain will achieve for me an eternal glory that far outweighs everything. This is Your promise to me. So, I fix my eyes not on what I see or feel, but on what is unseen. What is seen is temporary, but what is unseen is eternal in Your Kingdom.

In Jesus' name ... amen

REFLECTION QUESTIONS

1. God's timing is different than ours. How can you cultivate trust in God's timing, especially during seasons of pain or uncertainty, even when it feels like your prayers aren't being answered immediately?
2. In what areas of your life are you currently allowing fear or anxiety to take hold, and how can you actively choose to surrender these feelings to God, trusting in His strength and support?
3. We are to fix our eyes on what is unseen and eternal rather than what is temporary. How can you shift your focus from the temporary struggles or emotions you're facing to the eternal promises of God's Kingdom? What practical steps can you take to keep this perspective in your daily life?

_____

_____

_____

_____

_____

_____

_____

DECLARATIONS

1. Despite what I see in front of me, I will choose to trust God in this healing journey.
2. I will not let fear settle in my soul because God's perfect love casts out fear.
3. When having a pain-filled day, I will remind myself that you will achieve for me an eternal glory that outweighs everything I see in the natural.

SCRIPTURE REFERENCES

Psalm 56:8
Psalm 34:17
Psalm 46:1
Psalm 34:18
Isaiah 41:9-10
2 Cor 4:16-18

Journal/Notes: Pick one of the above scriptures, write it out and reflect on how you can put it into operation in your life today.

_____

_____

_____

_____

_____

_____

Prayers for When You Struggle With Rejection

Lord, there are moments when I feel so alone and rejected, as though no one understands or sees the pain in my heart. Yet, your Word reminds me that even if my father and mother forsake me, you will receive me. You are the One who holds me close when I feel abandoned and unseen. Thank you for being my refuge and strength, my ever-present help in times of trouble.

Jesus, you were despised and rejected by mankind, a man of sorrows, familiar with suffering. You know what it feels like to be misunderstood and cast aside. When the world hates me or when I face rejection, help me to remember that you experienced it first. You told us that if the world hates us, it hated you first. I find comfort knowing you understand my pain and walk with me through it.

You have commanded me not to fear, for you are with me. You are my God, who strengthens me, helps me, and upholds me with your righteous right hand. I choose to stand on your promises, trusting in your presence and power to carry me through whatever challenges or rejection I face.

If you are for me, Lord, who can be against me? Nothing and no one can separate me from your love. I claim that truth today. You are my light and my salvation—whom shall I fear? You are the stronghold of my life—of whom shall I be afraid?

Thank you, God, for being my constant, for loving me when I feel unworthy, and for reminding me that I am never truly alone. My confidence rests in you, my Protector, my Healer, and my Redeemer. In Jesus' name, I pray. Amen.

REFLECTION QUESTIONS

1. When you feel abandoned or rejected, how can you remind yourself that God has promised to receive and uphold you?
2. How does knowing that Jesus experienced rejection and suffering help you find comfort and strength in your own challenges?
3. What steps can you take to trust God's promise that He is with you, strengthening and helping you, even in the face of fear or opposition?

_____

_____

_____

_____

_____

_____

DECLARATIONS

1. I declare that even if others forsake me, the Lord will always receive and hold me close, for I am never alone in Him.
2. I declare that Jesus, who understands rejection and pain, walks with me and strengthens me in every challenge I face.
3. I declare that I will not fear, for God is my light, my salvation, and the stronghold of my life, and He is always for me.

SCRIPTURE REFERENCES

Psalm 27:10
Isaiah 53:3
John 15:18
Isaiah 41:10
Romans 8:31

Journal/Notes: Pick one of the above scriptures, write it out and reflect on how you can put it into operation in your life today.

_____
_____
_____
_____
_____
_____
_____

Prayers for When You Struggle With Shame

Lord, I am ready to shed the graveclothes of shame! I declare your Word over me that tells me that I am more than a conqueror through You because you love me. Neither death, nor life, angels or the enemy's principalities or their power have authority over me, in Jesus' Name! Nothing can separate me from your love.

I am so grateful that you have kept me out of the grave, and you declare me as your child. I am a royal priesthood! I am not disgraced or ashamed for you have put your mark, your stamp of approval on me. I will not allow fear to whisper the lies of my enemy into my soul. Jesus, forgive me for forgetting who I am in you. Holy Spirit, continue to sing my true identity over me.

It is written that I will not be put to shame and will not feel humiliated or ashamed for I will not be disgraced. No weapon forged against me will prosper and EVERY tongue that rises up against me will be condemned, in Jesus' name! Shame, be gone. You have no authority here.

In Jesus' mighty name!

Amen

REFLECTION QUESTIONS

1. How do you see yourself considering God's declaration over you? What steps can you take to

more fully embrace and live out your true identity in Christ, especially when faced with negative thoughts or external pressures?
2. What lies or negative beliefs have you been holding onto that contradict what God says about you? How can you actively reject these lies and replace them with the truth of God's Word?
3. In what areas of your life do you need to stand firm in the protection and authority that God has given you? How can you remind yourself of God's promises and declare them over your life when facing challenges or opposition?

_____

_____

_____

_____

_____

_____

DECLARATIONS

1. I choose to embrace my true identity in Christ, rejecting negative thoughts and external pressures that try to define me.
2. I cast down every lie that contradicts God's truth about me, replacing them with His Word, which declares that I am loved, chosen, and victorious.

3. I stand firm in the protection and authority God has given me, declaring His promises over every challenge and opposition I face."

SCRIPTURE REFERENCES

Romans 8:37-38
Psalms 30:3
Is. 45:17
Is. 54:4
Romans 10:11

Journal/Notes: Pick one of the above scriptures, write it out and reflect on how you can put it into operation in your life today.

_____

_____

_____

_____

_____

_____

_____

Prayers for When You're Weary of Crying

Heavenly Father, You know my tears and the burdens I carry. Your Word promises you have collected my tears in Your bottle and recorded them in Your book. I am weary from crying, but I hold onto the promise that You see ALL my tears, and none of them are wasted. I cling to the hope that You promise to wipe away every tear from my eyes, and there will be no more death, sorrow, or pain, for You are making all things new.

Amid my weariness, I look to You because You are my refuge and strength, a very present help in times of trouble. You are near to the broken-hearted, and You save those who are crushed. When my soul is faint, I remember that You satisfy the longing soul and fill the hungry soul with your goodness.

I will not fear, for You have chosen me and called me by name. You are with me. You strengthen me. You uphold me with Your righteous right hand, as You promised. Lord, I trust You to renew my strength and lift the weight of my tears. Thank You for Your unending comfort and faithfulness.

In Jesus' name, Amen.

REFLECTION QUESTIONS

1. How can you find comfort in knowing that God sees every tear and records your pain, even when you feel overwhelmed by weariness?

2. In what areas of your life can you rely more on God as your refuge and strength during times of trouble and sorrow?
3. Where are you struggling to believe that God is always with you and will strengthen you when you feel weak and burdened?

_____
_____
_____
_____
_____
_____
_____

DECLARATIONS

1. I declare that God has collected my tears and will comfort me, wiping away all sorrow as He makes all things new.
2. I declare that God is my refuge and strength, and I trust Him to sustain me in my weariness and restore my soul.
3. I declare that I am upheld by God's righteous right hand, and I will not fear, for He strengthens me and is always with me.

SCRIPTURE REFERENCES

Revelation 21:4-5
Psalm 107:19
Psalm 56:8
Psalm 9:9
Psalm 46:1
Isaiah 41:9-10

Journal/Notes: Pick one of the above scriptures, write it out and reflect on how you can put it into operation in your life today.

_____

_____

_____

_____

_____

_____

_____

PRAYERS FOR FAMILY

Prayers for When Your Children Need Healing

Heavenly Father, I come to You, asking for Your gentle hand of healing over my child. You see the pain that they carry, the confusion, and the questions in their heart. Lord, I ask that You reach into those tender places, bringing comfort, peace, and wholeness. Heal the wounds that divorce has left on their spirit, and let Your love fill every empty space.

I ask that You replace their hurt with hope, and any bitterness with the sweetness of Your grace. Strengthen their heart, Lord, and protect their mind from fear and anxiety. Remind them that they are deeply loved by You, that they are not defined by the brokenness they've witnessed, but by the beautiful future You have for them.

Give me wisdom, to be a source of love and stability for them. Let me speak words of life and encouragement, showing them that You are a refuge and a healer. Holy Spirit, help me to hold my tongue when I want to say something negative about my co-parent. Help me find words of life and appreciation for them.

Help me to lean on Your strength and to guide my child toward the security of Your promises. Thank You for being their perfect Father, the One who mends every heartache and restores all things.

In Jesus' name, Amen.

REFLECTION QUESTIONS

1. How can acknowledging God's role as the ultimate healer give you comfort over your child's healing?
2. In what ways might focusing on God's promises and faithfulness help shift your perspective on your child's future while healing from the divorce?
3. How can you model resilience and trust in God to help your child find peace and hope amid change?

_____

_____

_____

_____

_____

_____

_____

DECLARATIONS

1. I trust God to heal my child's heart and bring wholeness to their life.
2. I believe that God's love and grace are restoring my child's peace and hope.
3. I am a source of stability and strength for my child, relying on God to guide me.

SCRIPTURE REFERENCES

Jeremiah 30:17

Isaiah 53:5
Exodus 15:26
Jeremiah 17:14
Psalm 103:2-3
Psalm 30:2

Journal/Notes: Pick one of the above scriptures, write it out and reflect on how you can put it into operation in your life today.

_____

_____

_____

_____

_____

_____

_____

Prayers for When You Pray For Healing Over Your Former Spouse

Jesus, you know how much (spouse's name) hurt me. You know all the pain I carry; but your Word says if we don't forgive others, you won't forgive us. So even though I don't want to pray for them because of my pain; I know that is what you ask us to do.

Your Word says to bless those that persecute you, to bless and do not curse. So I choose to bless (spouse's name) with the blessings of the Lord. They belong to you, Jesus. If (spouse's name) needs healing, I ask that you heal them. If they need provision, make it so, Lord, by your mercy and grace.

I will choose to love (spouse's name) with the love of God and to bless them. Where possible and if safe to do so, I will do good to (spouse's name). And I will choose to pray for them even if they spitefully use me or persecute me. You know this is hard, Jesus, but I choose to do your will for I know you will bless my obedience.

If (spouse's name) has sinned against me, I choose to forgive him/her. Even if they sin against me seven times in a day; I will choose to forgive them. I recognize that it may not always feel like I have forgiven, but I don't do this out of feeling, but as a choice to put action to the Word of God in my life.

I choose to not avenge myself, for it is written that vengeance belongs to you. You promise to repay any sin against me. So, if (spouse's name) is hungry, I will feed them. If they are thirsty, I will give (spouse's name) a drink. I will overcome any evil done to me with good as it is safe to do so.

I commit (spouse's name) to you. Reveal your heart to them.

In Your Name, Jesus,

Amen

REFLECTION QUESTIONS

1. How do you demonstrate obedience to God's command to forgive, even when it feels difficult?
2. What role does the act of blessing your former spouse who has caused pain play in the healing process for you, and how might it reflect God's love to the other person?
3. How can you rely on God's justice and promises to overcome your desire for vengeance and choose good over evil in the divorce-relationship (if there is one needed)?

_____

_____

_____

_____

_____

_____

_____

DECLARATIONS

1. Even though it is difficult to pray blessings over (spouse's name), I will choose to do it as an act of obedience to the Lord.
2. I will work on actively choosing to speak kindly to (spouse's name), and about them to others.
3. I will overcome any evil done to me with good as it is safe to do so.

SCRIPTURE REFERENCES

Romans 12:14
Luke 6:27-28
Matthew 5:44
Luke 17:3-4
Romans 12:19-21

Journal/Notes: Pick one of the above scriptures, write it out and reflect on how you can put it into operation in your life today.

_____

_____

_____

_____

_____

_____

_____

Prayers for When You Worried About Your Children

Father, I come to You with my heart open and vulnerable, laying down my worries and fears about my children. I'm worried about how the divorce is affecting them. You know the deep love I have for them, and how often I carry the weight of their future, their safety, and their well-being. In moments when my thoughts turn anxious, remind me that You are the ultimate protector and guide, that You know their needs even better than I do, and that Your plans for them are good.

Lord, I ask for Your peace to wash over me. Help me to trust You more deeply, surrendering my concerns and placing them in Your capable hands. When I'm tempted to control every detail or speak negatively about my co-parent, remind me that Your wisdom and power are far greater than mine. Holy Spirit, remind me to release my grip and let You lead their steps, knowing You love them even more than I can comprehend.

Strengthen my heart to pray fervently for them, and to speak words of life, encouragement, and truth into their lives. Let me model a faith that they can see and follow, and let me lean on Your promises rather than my own understanding. Guard their hearts, protect their paths, and draw them closer to You.

Thank You, Father, for being a loving and faithful parent to us all. In You, I find peace, knowing that my children are safely held within Your care. Amen.

REFLECTION QUESTIONS

1. How might releasing control of your children's lives to God impact your perspective on daily anxieties?
2. In what ways can trusting God's wisdom provide comfort when worrying about the safety and future of your children?
3. How does modeling a life of faith and surrender benefit their children's spiritual growth and sense of security?

_____

_____

_____

_____

_____

_____

_____

DECLARATIONS

1. I trust God's plans for my children, knowing they are good and filled with hope.
2. I release my fears about my children to God, embracing His peace that surpasses all understanding.
3. I am a faithful example, relying on God's strength to lead and protect my family.

SCRIPTURE REFERENCES

Philippians 4:6-7
Jeremiah 29:11
Proverbs 3:5-6
Isaiah 41:10
Psalm 91:11

Journal/Notes: Pick one of the above scriptures, write it out and reflect on how you can put it into operation in your life today.

_____
_____
_____
_____
_____
_____
_____

PRAYERS FOR FORGIVENESS

Prayers for When Forgiveness Feels Impossible

Lord, sometimes it feels impossible to forgive (name here) _____. They brought so much hurt and destruction in my soul and life. Sometimes it feels like I am not able to do it within myself. But I want to walk free, I don't want to carry that certificate of offense and the weight of bitterness and resentment. It is weighing me down and wounding me. It is crippling my race to win the prize of Your upward call. I want to run free from this pain and heartache. So, help me be willing to forgive. Help me choose to take that first step toward healing.

And Lord, if needed, if that is still too hard of a step to take…help me be willing to be willing. Also, show me where I need to forgive myself for anything or ask for forgiveness from those who have hurt me.

Jesus, I want to let all bitterness, wrath, anger, clamor and evil speaking be put away from me. This is your mandate from heaven. Help me and strengthen me to be kind to _____ and others who have wounded me in this process. Show me how to be tender-hearted and forgive them because you forgave me of all my sins. Show me how to do this. I need your strength to forgive, let go, and run free.

In Jesus' name.

Amen

REFLECTION QUESTIONS

1. What does it mean to you to walk in forgiveness?
2. What does it mean to you to be *willing* to forgive? What areas of your life still need to be surrendered to Christ?
3. Whose name(s) are written on your certificate of offense?

_____

_____

_____

_____

_____

_____

_____

DECLARATIONS

1. I will not operate my life out of bitterness or anger. I choose to be kind, tender-hearted and walk in forgiveness.
2. I choose to walk a life of forgiveness.
3. In areas I am struggling to forgive, I choose to be willing to walk toward forgiveness, not away from it.

SCRIPTURE REFERENCES

Ephesians 4:31-32

Colossians 3:13
Matthew 6:14-15
Mark 11:25
Deut 32:35
2 Thess 1:6
Rom 12:19

Journal/Notes: Pick one of the above scriptures, write it out and reflect on how you can put it into operation in your life today.

_____

_____

_____

_____

_____

_____

_____

Prayers for When You're Offended With God

Oh, Heavenly Father, I am SO grateful that you are slow to anger and abound in steadfast love. You forgive every iniquity and transgression; at the same time, you tell me that YOU will avenge and take care of any wrongdoing. It is hard to lay this on your alter and walk away. It is hard to trust you to take care of it. But I choose to yield control over to you. I am SO thankful that you do not deal with me according to my sins, and you do not repay me according to my mistakes.

Jesus, you are forgiving and good. You abound in love to all You call your own. Help me to let go and let you handle it. Help me to relinquish my right to my pain and turn it over to you. I want to walk free from offense and all the pain that comes with it.

You are merciful and forgiving, even if I have rebelled against you. It is written that if I confess my sins, you are faithful and just to forgive me my sins and you will cleanse me from all unrighteousness. I am truly sorry for holding offense against you. Show me any areas that I am hiding fault with you. I choose, today, to lay down my rights to this pain. I choose to forgive you and let you heal these wounds.

Thank you for the healing work You are starting in me. Thank you for your forgiveness and giving me the strength to lay this down at Your feet and walk away. Remind me to do this every time I choose to pick it up again.

REFLECTION QUESTIONS

1. Have you ever found yourself offended with God? How did it impact your faith journey?
2. What steps can you take to begin the process of forgiving God and healing from past hurts?
3. How can changing your perspective from what God does to who God is affect your faith and relationship with Him?

_____

_____

_____

_____

_____

_____

_____

DECLARATIONS

1. I release any offense I've held toward God, choosing to trust His goodness and embrace healing for my heart.
2. I forgive God for what I did not understand, knowing His plans are higher than mine and His love for me never fails.
3. I shift my focus from what God *does* to who He *is*, anchoring my faith in His unchanging nature and endless grace.

SCRIPTURE REFERENCES

Ephesians 4:31-32
Numbers 14:18
Psalm 103:10–12
Psalm 86:5
Daniel 9:9
1 John 1:9

Journal/Notes: Pick one of the above scriptures, write it out and reflect on how you can put it into operation in your life today.

_____

_____

_____

_____

_____

_____

Prayers for When Unforgiveness Feels Good

Jesus, it seems impossible to forgive those that have hurt me. I don't know how to do it by myself. Holy Spirit, I invite you to show me how to do this! Help me to forgive my debtors as you have forgiven them. I want and need your forgiveness, Jesus, so show me how to forgive and release them.

I don't want any barriers between you and me! I do not want to foster bitterness, wrath, and anger. I want it to be put away from me. Help me to be kind to those that wound me, help me to be tender-hearted toward any wounds they carry.

I can only do this through Christ who strengthens me! Holy Spirit, you have permission to tap me on the shoulder when I pick up unforgiveness like an old friend. I want your love, joy, peace, and healing in my life and in my body. And it starts with me being willing and able to forgive to completion. I stand before the Lord today and choose to forgive. Help me and remind me to do this every day until forgiveness has had its complete work in in me.

I pray this in Jesus' name,

Amen

REFLECTION QUESTIONS

1. What specific steps can you take today to begin the process of forgiving someone who has hurt you deeply?
2. In what areas of your life do you sense bitterness, wrath, or anger, and how can you invite the Holy Spirit to help you release these emotions?
3. How can you cultivate a tender heart towards those who have wounded you, allowing Christ's strength to guide your actions and thoughts?

_____

_____

_____

_____

_____

_____

_____

DECLARATIONS

1. I choose to forgive those who have hurt me because Christ has forgiven them. This is a choice of my will and I know the feelings will follow.
2. I choose to walk in the Love of God toward those who have hurt me, even when it is hard.
3. I choose to let go of my right to carry offense. I lay it at the foot of the cross and walk away.

SCRIPTURE REFERENCES

Matthew 6:12, (ESV)
Matthew 6:14-15, (ESV
Ephesians 4:31-32, (ESV
Philippians 4:13, (ESV)
Galatians 5:22-23

Journal/Notes: Pick one of the above scriptures, write it out and reflect on how you can put it into operation in your life today.

_____

_____

_____

_____

_____

_____

_____

Prayers for When Want to Take Justice Into Your Own Hands

Lord, you know the pains and the secret pains I carry. You know the burden of betrayal, and my desire for that justice to come out like a white knight on a horse and slay the dragon for me. I know you reveal the deeply secret things. I know that you know what is really in the darkness. I repent for wanting to bring my former spouse's secrets out into the light as a form of verbal "justice."

And Lord, when the sentence or the justice for the crimes committed against me are not carried out quickly, I want to take this into my own hands. Forgive me. And Lord, if _____ does not know you, I ask that you reveal the condition of their heart to them. Bring them into alignment with repentance and the grace and mercy of Your Word.

I know You love justice. I know You hate robbery and any wrong thing, and Your Word says that You will faithfully give them their recompense. It is Your desire that everybody come to repentance and seek You and healing through You. Therefore, Lord, I will wait. I will choose to wait for Your justice. I will choose to wait for You to reveal the hidden things in the darkness and bring everything out into the light.

Holy Spirit remind me that I have made this choice, and that I have consecrated my heart to this. Remind me that You are in control, and that You will bring everything to justice in Your time.

In Jesus' name Amen.

REFLECTION QUESTIONS

1. What steps can you take to surrender your need for immediate justice and rely on God's perfect plan?
2. What hidden desires for revenge or verbal justice are you holding onto?
3. In what ways can you deepen your faith and remind yourself that God is working, even when justice is not immediately visible?

_____

_____

_____

_____

_____

_____

_____

DECLARATIONS

1. I choose to trust God's perfect timing and release my desire for immediate justice, knowing He will bring everything into the light.
2. I choose to walk in grace and forgiveness, resisting the temptation to reveal or expose others' wrongs out of revenge.
3. The Holy Spirit strengthens me to wait patiently, reminding me that God is in control and will faithfully bring justice according to His plan.

SCRIPTURE REFERENCES

Ecclesiastes 8:11-13, NIV
Ecclesiastes 12:13-14 NIV
Isaiah 30:18
Isaiah 61:8
Romans 12:19 NIV
Mark 4:22
Daniel 2:22

Journal/Notes: Pick one of the above scriptures, write it out and reflect on how you can put it into operation in your life today.

_____

_____

_____

_____

_____

_____

PRAYERS FOR IDENTITY

Prayers for When You Don't Remember Who You Are

Jesus, I feel lost. I don't remember who I was before marriage and divorce. It was as if I dissolved like cotton candy in water. As I sit amid the divorce debris, I choose to awake and reclaim what your Word says about me. It is written that if anyone is in Christ, they are a new creation. The old has passed away; behold, the new has come.

I have been crucified with Christ. It is no longer I who live, but Christ who lives in me. And the life I now live in the flesh I choose to live by faith in the Son of God, who loved me and gave himself for me. I choose to step into this new season as a new creation. Jesus has called me out of darkness and into His light! I am His workmanship and not the product of divorce.

God has not given me a spirit of fear, but of love, power and a sound mind. I speak the name of Jesus over my heart and mind and declare the healing work He provided on the Christ over me and my future. I am His child, the apple of His eye, and my new life is hidden in Christ.

In this wilderness season where silence and chaos compete for my attention, I choose to fix my eyes on Jesus and what He says about me, not what those around me say. Jesus, continue to show me how You see me.

In your mighty name,

Amen

REFLECTION QUESTIONS

1. How can you reclaim your identity in Christ and let go of the labels and identities formed during marriage and divorce?
2. In what ways can you actively live out the truth that you are a new creation, stepping out of darkness and into the light of Jesus?
3. When silence and chaos compete for your attention, how can you remain grounded in what Jesus says about you?

_____
_____
_____
_____
_____
_____
_____

DECLARATIONS

1. I release the labels of my past and reclaim my identity in Christ, embracing who God says I am.
2. I am a new creation in Christ, and I will boldly walk in His light, leaving behind the darkness of my past.

3. Amid silence or chaos, I remain grounded in God's truth—I am chosen, loved, and secure in Jesus.

SCRIPTURE REFERENCES

2 Corinthians 5:17
Galatians 2:20
1 Peter 2:9
Ephesians 2:10
2 Timothy 1:7
John 1:12
Colossians 3:3

Journal/Notes: Pick one of the above scriptures, write it out and reflect on how you can put it into operation in your life today.

_____

_____

_____

_____

_____

_____

Prayers for When You Feel Disqualified

Father, thank You for Your unfailing grace. Thank You that Your calling is not revoked by my mistakes. Lord, I battle with feeling disqualified and ashamed because of my past. Remind my soul and spirit that Your love is constant, and Your anointing remains. Give me the strength to rise and reclaim their purpose, knowing that You work all things together for good.

You tell me in your Word that Your gifts and call are irrevocable. My call is not due to any perfection on my part. You bestow on me a crown of beauty instead of the ashes of divorce. You give me the oil of joy instead of mourning, and a garment of praise instead of a spirit of despair. I remind my soul that Your grace is sufficient for me, for Your power is made perfect in weakness. Therefore, I will boast even more gladly about my weaknesses, so that Christ's power may rest on me.

I am so thankful that you do not look at things that people do. People look at the outward appearance, but the Lord looks at the heart. It is written in Proverbs that though the righteous fall seven times, they rise again…" and in Jesus' name I will rise again!

I present these ashes for your glory, Amen.

REFLECTION QUESTIONS

1. In what areas are you carrying the ashes of your divorce? Is it ashes of bitterness? Shame?

2. Is there a dream you have laid down because you feel disqualified due to your divorce?
3. Do you have any areas of sin that you feel are keeping you from stepping out in your call? Confess them to the Lord and to a trusted friend. Get wise counsel from someone you trust.

_____

_____

_____

_____

_____

_____

_____

DECLARATIONS

1. God has given me a crown of beauty for my ashes. I have the oil of joy instead of mourning and a garment of praise. Despair has no place in me!
2. Christ's grace is sufficient for me and His power is made perfect in my weakness.
3. Though I have fallen many times in my life, I will rise again! I will not sit in defeat.

SCRIPTURES

Romans 11:29
Isaiah 61:3

2 Corinthians 12:9
1 Samuel 1:7
Proverbs 24:16

Journal/Notes: Pick one of the above scriptures, write it out and reflect on how you can put it into operation in your life today.

_____

_____

_____

_____

_____

_____

_____

Prayers for When You Struggle to Accept God's Love

Lord, I know you love me, but I am really struggling to accept it as mine. I don't understand this concept of unconditional love. Your Word says that we should love because you first loved us. Help me to understand this. I know that you died for me. I know that you sent your one and only Son into the world that we might live through Him. This is love: not that we loved God, but that He loved us and sent his Son as an atoning sacrifice for our sins.

I want to embrace this as my new identity: totally loved unconditionally. Help me understand that even though you died for all, that this also applies to me. Reveal your heart to me! Help me hear your heartbeat. Wrap your arms and heart around me and help me feel this love you paid for with your very life. It is written that if anyone is in Christ, they are a new creation. The old has gone away and the new is here. So, until I feel it, I will claim it by faith in you.

I know, according to your Word that there is no condemnation for those that are in Christ. By faith I claim that I am God's chosen, holy and dearly loved! I will clothe myself with your compassion, kindness, humility, gentleness and patience. I will work towards bearing with others and forgiving when I have unforgiveness toward another; for I know that if I harbor unforgiveness toward anyone, that I cannot truly embrace your love. I will learn to forgive as you forgave, and I will put on your love which binds me with others in perfect unity.

God, you so loved the world and gave your one and only Son, so that whoever believes in Him shall not perish but have eternal life. Thank you for your sacrifice for *me* because you love *me*.

In Jesus' name,

Amen

REFLECTION QUESTIONS

1. What barriers in your heart or mind make it difficult for you to fully accept God's unconditional love for you, and how can you surrender those to Him?
2. How can you actively embrace your identity as a new creation in Christ and live in the truth that there is no condemnation for those in Him?
3. In what ways can you demonstrate God's love by forgiving others and living with compassion, kindness, and humility, even when it is challenging?

_____

_____

_____

_____

_____

_____

DECLARATIONS

1. I declare that I am fully loved by God, unconditionally and personally, and I choose to receive His love as my identity.
2. I am a new creation in Christ; the old has passed away, and there is no condemnation for me because I am in Him.
3. I will clothe myself with compassion, kindness, humility, gentleness, and patience, forgiving others as Christ has forgiven me, and walking in His perfect love.

SCRIPTURE REFERENCES

Romans 8:1
1 John 4:19
1 John 4:9-11
2 Corinthians 5:14-17
Colossians 3:12-14
John 3:16

Journal/Notes: Pick one of the above scriptures, write it out and reflect on how you can put it into operation in your life today.

_____
_____
_____
_____
_____

Prayers for When You Struggle With Your Identity in Christ

Lord, I know I am more than a divorce certificate! You sealed my identity long before the divorce. You love me and have an amazing destiny planned for me. Upon my conception, my identity is assured and etched in Your heart. Divorce did not change that. You knew me and my destiny even *before* You formed me in the womb! As I declare your word, help it remind me of my true worth and identity in You.

Jesus, it is written that I am YOUR workmanship, and I'm created in Christ for good works. You have prepared all of that before I even started walking with you. I will NOT fear because You, Lord, have redeemed me. You call me by my name, and I am yours. Hallelujah! I am a child of God because I believe in His name.

You knew me even before you formed me in the womb, and you sanctified me even then. You chose me as an adopted child according to your will. Thank you, Lord. Your Word says that I am one with you. Reveal this to my heart and spirit and help me understand it at a deeper level. Thank you for choosing me in this generation as your royal priesthood and your own special child. I will proclaim the praises of my Jesus because you call me out of darkness and into your marvelous, glorious light!

Thank you, Lord. In Your name,

Amen

REFLECTION QUESTIONS

1. How does recognizing that your identity was established before your divorce impact the way you see yourself today?
2. What steps can you take to deepen your understanding of being God's workmanship and walking in the good works He prepared for you?
3. In what areas of your life do you need to proclaim God's Word more boldly, knowing you are part of His royal priesthood and chosen for a purpose?

_____

_____

_____

_____

_____

_____

_____

DECLARATIONS

1. My identity is not defined by divorce or circumstances—I am who God says I am, chosen and sealed in His love from the beginning.
2. I am God's workmanship, created in Christ for good works, and I will walk boldly in the purpose He prepared for me.

3. I am a child of God, called out of darkness into His marvelous light, and I will proclaim His goodness in every area of my life.

SCRIPTURE REFERENCES

Ephesians 2:10
Isaiah 43:1
John 1:12
Jeremiah 1:5
Ephesians 1:5
1 Corinthians 6:17
1 Peter 2:9

Journal/Notes: Pick one of the above scriptures, write it out and reflect on how you can put it into operation in your life today.

_____
_____
_____
_____
_____
_____
_____

PRAYERS FOR SPIRITUAL WARFARE

Prayers for Recovery After Abuse

Lord, I come to You broken and weary. I am battle worn. It is written in Your Word that you are faithful, and you will establish and guard me and my family from the evil one. I need You to come to my/our defense. Holy Spirit, breathe your life into me to so I can lift the sword of the Spirit to declare to the heavenlies because you are for me/us, so who can be against me/us!

Even though I am weary, You promise to arm me with strength for the battle and You will subdue under me those who rise up against me. Help me see into the spirit what is coming against me/us. Because I call You, Jesus, my Savior, You give me the authority to trample on serpents and scorpions and over all the power of the enemy. Nothing by any means will hurt me/us. That doesn't mean the attacks will stop; but it does mean that you draw a Blood line around us/me.

I speak to my weary soul and remind myself to dwell in the secret place of the Most High. I will abide under the shadow of my Almighty God. For He is my/our refuge and fortress. I choose to put my trust in God. He will cover me/us with His feathers and under His wings take refuge. I declare that by His Stripes I/we are healed in Jesus' Name.

Jesus, I love you. Show me your glory and your wisdom as I navigate this season. Heal me/us and strengthen me/us. Bring Divine appointments to others who can help me/us heal.

In Jesus' name

Amen

REFLECTION QUESTIONS

1. How can you rely on God's promises to renew your strength when you feel battle-worn and weary? What specific scriptures or affirmations help you the most during these times?
2. Reflect on how you can use the spiritual authority given to you through Christ. What practical steps can you take to remain vigilant against spiritual challenges while healing and trusting in God's protection?
3. In what ways can you intentionally dwell in the "secret place of the Most High?" How can trusting in God as your refuge and fortress shape your responses to current struggles?

_____

_____

_____

_____

_____

_____

_____

DECLARATIONS

1. Even when I am weary, I choose to lift the Sword of the Spirit -- the Word of God and pray and declare it over me and my family.
2. I choose to dwell in the secret place with Jesus instead of doing the battle on my own.
3. Even when there is chaos around me, I will choose to act out of the spirit and not my flesh.

SCRIPTURE REFERENCES

2 Thessalonians 3:3
Romans 8:31
Psalm 18:39
Luke 10:19
Psalm 91
Isaiah 53:5

Journal/Notes: Pick one of the above scriptures, write it out and reflect on how you can put it into operation in your life today.

_____

_____

_____

_____

_____

_____

_____

Prayers for When You Need To War For Your Children

It is written in Your Word that I do not walk in the flesh; nor do I war in the flesh. The weapons of my warfare are not carnal but mighty in God for the pulling down of strongholds over my children. In Jesus Name, I will cast down every argument and high thing that exalts itself against the knowledge of God in my family. I choose to bring all my thoughts into the captivity and obedience of Christ.

With this authority of my identity in Christ, I claim a Blood line of protection around my child/children. Jesus, you have armed me as their parent with Your strength for the battles ahead. Your Word promises that you have subdued those who rise up against me or my family. He who is in me is greater than he that is in this world.

My family dwells in the secret place of the Most High and we will abide under the shadow of the Almighty God for He is our refuge and our fortress. I choose to trust Him. Because I have made the Lord my refuge and the Most High God my dwelling place, no evil shall befall me or my children. In Jesus' name, no plague will come near our dwelling.

Lord, you will give your angels charge over my child/children and will keep them in all your ways. In their hands they will bear them up lest they dash their foot against a stone. You have set your love upon my family and will deliver them. You promise to be with us in trouble. You promise to deliver us and honor us as we honor you.

Jesus, show your salvation to my children. Show them how much you love and cherish them. Reveal your heart to them as they sleep and go about their day. Watch over them. I entrust them into your care.

In the powerful name of Jesus,

Amen

REFLECTION QUESTIONS

1. How can embracing your authority in Christ impact the way you approach challenges within your family?
2. What does it mean for you to make the Lord your refuge and dwelling place, especially when facing fears or uncertainties for your children?
3. How can you actively demonstrate trust in God's promises for protection and guidance over your children in your daily life?

_____

_____

_____

_____

_____

_____

_____

DECLARATIONS

1. Because of my authority in Christ, I have the power and authority to pull down strongholds of the enemy.
2. Jesus Christ is my refuge, and I trust Him to watch over my child/children.
3. You have set your love upon my family, and you will save them.

SCRIPTURE REFERENCES

Psalm 18:39
Psalm 91
1 John 4:4
2 Corinthians 10:3-5

Journal/Notes: Pick one of the above scriptures, write it out and reflect on how you can put it into operation in your life today.

_____

_____

_____

_____

_____

_____

_____

Prayers for When You Need to War Over Your Heart

Lord, I give you praise and thanks because, according to your Word, you give me victory through my Lord, Jesus Christ. I relinquish my heart and all its hurts to you. I kneel at your footstool and lay them at your feet. (Name the hurts you are laying at His feet. Be specific).

Lord, you know these have wounded my heart, but I choose not to harbor this pain and allow the enemy to use it. You are faithful and you will establish truth and guard me from the evil one. I am so thankful that you arm me with Your truth and Your strength for the battle for my heart. It is written that you have subdued under me those things/people/attitudes that rose up against me.

I come against the spirit behind these hurts and offenses. Even though these have wounded me, I will not allow the enemy to use them as tools to keep me in bitterness and offense. In Jesus' name, I renounce these (name them) hurts and the power that they have had up until today. In Jesus' name I break their power over my heart. My heart belongs to Christ, and I will stand upon His Word.

I choose to put on the whole armor of God, and I will stand against the wiles of the devil. I recognize that I do not wrestle against flesh and blood, but against principalities, powers, and the rulers of the darkness of this age. I wrestle against spiritual *hosts* of wickedness in the heavenly *places*. Therefore, I will take up the whole armor of God, that I am be able to withstand in the evil day, and having done all, to stand upon the truth of God's Word.

In Jesus' name, I will gird my waist with His truth. I put on the breastplate of righteousness and cover my feet with the gospel of peace. Above all, I will take the shield of faith, and I will be able to quench all the fiery darts of the wicked one. I will take the helmet of salvation, and the sword of the Spirit, which is the Word of God.

Jesus, Your Word declares that I have peace even when I don't feel it. Lately, I feel only tribulation, chaos and pain in this world. But, it is written that You have overcome the world. Hallelujah!! Thank you for the victory that is mine. Thank You for guarding me. Thank You for arming me with Your Word.

In Jesus' mighty name,

Amen

REFLECTION QUESTIONS

1. What specific hurts or offenses are you being called to release to God today, and how can surrendering these lead to healing and freedom?
2. How can recognizing that your battle is not against flesh and blood, but spiritual forces, shift the way you respond to pain and conflict?
3. Which piece of the armor of God (truth, righteousness, faith, peace, salvation, or the Word) feels most essential to you right now, and how can you intentionally put it on in your daily walk?

DECLARATIONS

1. I am under the authority of Christ and His Word. My hurts will not rule me.
2. Even though I don't always feel the peace of God, I decare to my body and soul that Jesus overcame the world and that is where my peace is found.
3. I choose to recognize the battle is not against flesh and blood; but against powers and principalities that are trying to control my heart.

SCRIPTURE REFERENCES

Psalm 18:39
1 Corinthians 15:57
2 Thessalonians 3:3
John 16:33
Ephesians 6:11-17

Journal/Notes: Pick one of the above scriptures, write it out and reflect on how you can put it into operation in your life today.

_____

_____

_____

_____

_____

_____

_____

Prayers for When You Need To War For Your Future

Jesus, my future belongs to you. No weapon formed against it shall prosper and every tongue that rises up in judgment against my future will be condemned. My righteousness comes from the Almighty God, not man. It says in Your Word that you have armed me with strength for any battle. In Jesus name, subdue any who come against my future and all the plans you have for me.

I put on the whole armor of God, so I may stand against the wiles of the devil. For I do not wrestle against flesh and blood, but against principalities, against powers, against the rulers of the darkness of this age. I wrestle against spiritual *hosts* of wickedness in the heavenly places. So, I will take up the whole armor of God, that I may be able to withstand in the evil day, and having done all, to stand on Your Word.

I will gird my waist with truth and put on the breastplate of Christ's righteousness. I have shod my feet with the preparation of the gospel of peace. And above all, I take the shield of faith with which I will be able to quench all the fiery darts of the wicked one that come against my future. And I put on the helmet of salvation, and pick up the sword of the Spirit, which is the Word of God.

It is written that if I resist the devil, he will flee from me. The Lord God is my sun and shield and will give me the grace and glory to step into the future He has for me. The Word says that the Lord will not withhold any good thing from those who walk uprightly.

Jesus, bring Divine appointments, friends and mentors who can help me walk uprightly in this season ahead.

In Jesus' mighty name!

Amen

REFLECTION QUESTIONS

1. How can you deepen your trust in God's promises for your future, especially in the face of challenges or spiritual battles? What does relying on His righteousness over human validation mean to you personally?
2. Which piece of the armor of God do you feel most equipped with in this season, and which might need more focus or strengthening?
3. Reflect on how you can remain open to God's divine appointments and guidance. What steps can you take to surround yourself with godly mentors and friends who will encourage you to walk uprightly in alignment with His plans?

_____

_____

_____

_____

_____

_____

DECLARATIONS

1. I will daily choose to take up the armor of God so I can withstand any attack that comes my way.
2. I will trust the Lord with my future and choose to let Him draw up the map. I will not draw my own map and choose my own way.
3. I will choose to resist the devil and all the wiles that he puts in front of me to get me off course.

SCRIPTURE REFERENCES

Psalm 84:11
Isaiah 54:17
James 4:7
Psalm 18:39
Ephesians 6:11-17

Journal/Notes: Pick one of the above scriptures, write it out and reflect on how you can put it into operation in your life today.

Prayers for When You Need to Build Boundaries Around Your Heart

Lord, I come to you with my broken heart. I have given my heart to many things and have not allowed you to protect it by building Godly walls around it. Please forgive me. Teach me how to keep my heart focused and committed to you with all diligence, for I know that out of it spring the issues of my life. I have gone in the way that seemed right in my own eyes, but you have weighed my heart. I long to go the way that is right in your eyes.

I choose to put on the whole armor of God so I can build Godly walls and stand against the enemy. I do not wrestle against flesh and blood, but against the things of this world that are filled with darkness. I will bind myself to Your truth and put on Your breastplate of righteousness. I will cover my feet with the gospel of peace and pick up the shield of faith so I can extinguish the fiery darts of the enemy. I choose to wear the helmet of salvation and pick up my spiritual sword which is Your Word.

It is written in your Word that you have armed me with strength for battles even when I don't feel strong. You are strong in me and my identity is in You. You promise to subdue those who rise up against me. Your Word promises that I have peace in You, even if I don't feel it. So, reveal this peace to me. Show me where my peace is when I am anxious or concerned. You tell me to be of good cheer because you have overcome the world. So, I stand on that firm foundation.

Holy Spirit, I give you permission to show me when I have stepped out of the protection of my identity in Christ. Show me when my heart is unprotected.

In Jesus' name,

Amen

REFLECTION QUESTIONS

1. In what ways have you given your heart to things that pull you away from God's protection, and how can you realign your heart to focus on Him with all diligence?
2. What steps can you take daily to "put on the full armor of God" and stand against the enemy's attacks on your mind, heart, and peace?
3. How can you become more aware when you've stepped outside the protection of your identity in Christ, and what role does the Holy Spirit play in guiding you back?

_____

_____

_____

_____

_____

_____

_____

DECLARATIONS

1. I choose to keep my heart under God's care and not my own.
2. I choose to put on the whole armor of God to withstand the tactics of the enemy.
3. Before I commit my heart to anything or anyone, I will make sure it is in keeping with God's Word.

SCRIPTURE REFERENCES

Ephesians 6:11-17
John 16:33
Psalm 18:39
Proverbs 4:23
Proverbs 21:2

Journal/Notes: Pick one of the above scriptures, write it out and reflect on how you can put it into operation in your life today.

_____

_____

_____

_____

_____

_____

Prayers for When You Need To Engage in Spiritual Warfare

In the name of Jesus, I stand boldly in Your authority against every force that seeks to come against me. I declare that I am a child of God, covered by the blood of Jesus, and no weapon formed against me shall prosper. I take my place in the spiritual battle, clothed in Your armor, and I refuse to be moved by fear, doubt, or intimidation.

I rebuke every lie, every scheme, and every attack that the enemy has sent my way. I break the power of any words or thoughts that I have uttered or that others have uttered against me that do not align with Your truth. I declare that my mind is protected by Your peace, my heart is guarded by Your righteousness, and my steps are directed by Your wisdom. Greater is He who is in me than he who is in the world!

In the authority of Jesus Christ, I claim victory over every area of my life. I speak healing, strength, and freedom over my body, my mind, and my spirit. The enemy has no power here, and I declare that the Lord is my refuge, my fortress, and my deliverer. Thank You, Father, that I am more than a conqueror through You.

In Jesus' mighty name, Amen.

REFLECTION QUESTIONS

1. What areas of life can you actively declare victory over by standing in God's authority and His Word?

2. How can focusing on being "more than a conqueror" in Christ shift your approach to spiritual battles?
3. What are practical ways to reject fear and reinforce God's truth when facing challenges?

___

DECLARATIONS

1. I stand in the authority of Jesus Christ, and no weapon formed against me shall prosper.
2. I am more than a conqueror, and I claim victory over every area of my life.
3. I am protected, healed, and strengthened by God's power, and the enemy has no hold on me.

SCRIPTURE REFERENCES

Jeremiah 30:17
Isaiah 53:5
Exodus 15:26
Jeremiah 17:14
Psalm 103:2-3

Psalm 30:2

Journal/Notes: Pick one of the above scriptures, write it out and reflect on how you can put it into operation in your life today.

_____

_____

_____

_____

_____

_____

_____

A Free Resource for You

You have a calling and a destiny! The promises of God throughout the Bible didn't stop being yours when you went through a divorce, despite what church leadership or well- meaning Christians may have said. Your destiny does not stop because you are divorced!

This resource will help you re-remember who and whose you are. In this book are scriptures and lessons to show you that:

Rest assured, your destiny is guaranteed. It is time to rise, reclaim, rebuild, and let Him restore your life again.

https://dl.bookfunnel.com/4k769kpebf

About the Author

A Journey From Seven to Redemption

When I was seven, my innocent proclamation to my Chatty Kathy doll set the stage for a lifelong journey. "That's IT!" I declared, typing out the best-selling book title, "Kids Have Rights Too." In hindsight, my mother probably just asked me to clean my room. But little did I know that this childish declaration would serve as a prophetic call to my inner soul. The dream of writing something profound and world-changing lingered, shaping the course of my life.

As an adult, the church was my refuge during the aftermath of childhood sexual abuse. However, during a soul-ripping divorce, the same church became a porcupine of well-intentioned but judgmental "scriptural advice." I was the minister's wife, bearing the weight of pain behind a smile and scripture, hiding the struggles to maintain an image of unwavering leadership. Yet, the breaking point came when stroke-like symptoms manifested, and I woke up with a resolute "Enough!" The journey to rediscover and reclaim my identity in Christ began.

Early Challenges: Navigating the Uncharted Territory

While crawling on the road to recovery, I noticed a gap in resources for those facing divorce within the Christian community. Despite the plethora of books on divorce, there was little on healing from both the separation and the judgment of church peers. The struggle to rebuild identity as God's "divorced" child was real, and I found myself yearning for guidance on my continued purpose in His Kingdom.

Our Mission: Rise, Reclaim, Redeem and Step Out

Like many, I refuse to be confined by the typical mainstream church's anti-divorce narrative. Pressing my face like flint into the sandstorm of divorce, I rediscovered the Cross, embracing my remembered and redeemed identity as His daughter. My mission is clear: to encourage, inspire, and ignite divorced individuals in the church to rise and take their place in the destiny God has set before them.

This mission is rooted in the belief that God isn't done with us just because our marriages ended. I've walked through fear, shame, loss, and depression, thinking my dreams shattered with the judge's stamp on that divorce certificate. If this sounds familiar, know that you are not alone. I want to partner with you to rise, reclaim, and redeem your identity, stepping into your call in Christ.

The Future: A Vision of Redemption

If you're ready to rise, reclaim, and step into your call, join our like-minded community. Sign up for our monthly newsletter, featuring articles inspiring you to break out of the box you've been placed in. I will also be highlighting books and resources that encouraged and ignited my desire to climb out of the pit I found myself in.

As a gift, I offer you a free ebook: "*Who Am I After Divorce*?" This guide includes specific scriptures to pray over yourself, a tool that played a pivotal role in my healing journey. By downloading it, you're staking a claim and taking a step toward your healing. The journey may be challenging, but together, we can rediscover and reclaim our identities, and make a difference in the world.

Where to find Dana L. Wiliams and Redeemed-Identity

Website: www.redeemed-identity.com

Find me on Social Media:
https://www.facebook.com/redeemidentity/

https://www.instagram.com/redeemidentity

My Free ebook, "Who Am I After Divorce?" can be downloaded here:
https://dl.bookfunnel.com/4k769kpebf

Website and Blog link:
https://redeemed-identity.com/blog/

Where to find Redeemed Identity After Divorce Podcast:

Apple: https://podcasts.apple.com/us/podcast/rise-reclaim-and-step-out-after-divorce-christian/id1752761447

Website: https://redeemed-identity.com/podcast

www.ingramcontent.com/pod-product-compliance
Lightning Source LLC
Chambersburg PA
CBHW020940090426
42736CB00010B/1210